A Guide to

CALIFORNIA'S HISTORIC SITES & MUSEUMS

San Francisco CVB GOLDEN GATE BRIDGE

AN AMERICAN TRAVELER SERIES PUBLICATION

Deborah Dinzes

2008 Printing

ISBN-13: 978-1-55838-134-6
ISBN-10: 1-55838-134-1

American Traveler Press
A Division of Primer Publishers
5738 North Central Avenue
Phoenix, Arizona 85012
www.AmericanTravelerPress.com
1-800-521-9221

Cover photo of State Capitol courtesy of California Department of Parks & Recreation. All interior photos by author, unless otherwise noted.

10 9 8 7 6 5 4
Printed in China. Published in the United States of America.

WELCOME

The settlement of California played an important role in the development of our nation. It was here that the dream of "Manifest Destiny" became a reality.

The land was originally inhabited by hundreds of small clans of Native Americans. In 1542, Juan Cabrillo landed at San Diego, claiming the territory for Spain. In 1579, Sir Frances Drake explored to the northern coast. In 1602, Sebastian Viscaino landed at Monterey, raising the Spanish Flag and reaffirming Spanish claims. Europeans first settled in California in the 1770s, establishing royal *presidios* (forts) at San Diego, Santa Barbara, Monterey, and San Francisco. The settlement process was augmented by the efforts of Father Junipero Serra, who founded a chain of Franciscan missions along the coast. By the 1780s, *pueblos* (towns) had been established from San Diego to San Francisco.

Following Mexican independence from Spain in 1822, California came under Mexican rule, although the province remained virtually autonomous. The missions were secularized and church holdings were given to prominent Mexican families in huge land grants. Up north, the numbers of American homesteaders increased rapidly as rumors of "Golden California" made their way back east.

War finally broke out between Mexico and the United States in 1846. Except for a few skirmishes in the south, there was almost no fighting between the Californians and American troops. On July 7, 1846, Commodore John Sloat raised the American Flag above Monterey. California became the 31st state in the union on September 9, 1850.

Meanwhile the most important event in California's settlement was occurring: The Gold Rush of 1849. It permanently altered the character of the state and had a profound effect on the nation. Millions of people from around the world raced to California, and many stayed. Indeed, the lure of the Golden State has never subsided. The state's population increases every year with people seeking their own El Dorado.

Nearly half of the United State's designated historic sites and many of its leading museums are in California. When traveling, look for light brown "Historical Site" signs posted along the highways that direct travelers to places of interest.

California's Historic Sites & Museums is part of the American Traveler Series. There are other related titles you should know about:

California Missions—A Guide to the State's Spanish Heritage
Ghost Towns of California—Remnants of the Mining Days
Railroads of California—Seeing the State by Rail

Contents

Santa Catalina Island Co. AVALON BAY & CASINO

HEARST SAN SIMEON STATE HISTORICAL MONUMENT

From a distance, The Castle on La Cuesta Encantada looks almost dreamlike. Huge Mediterranean-style turrets, a massive granite facade, and rows of palm trees give travelers the impression of a Californian Alhambra. It is, of course, the home of publisher William Randolph Hearst.

The 127-acre estate, located on the Pacific Coast Highway north of San Luis Obispo, overlooks San Simeon, the Pacific Ocean, and the Santa Lucia mountains. It includes a 115-room main residence, three guesthouses, two pools, and extensive gardens.

Hearst Castle houses millions of dollar's worth of art collections, antiques and antiquities. The main residence, La Casa Grande, is filled with Spanish and Italian antiques and art, gothic tapestries, and silver. It is one of the world's most extensive private collections.

Ellis/Sawyer Hearst San Simeon S.H.M. NEPTUNE POOL, HEARST CASTLE

William Randolph Hearst was born in San Francisco in 1863. In 1865, his gold-and-silver mine-wealthy father purchased several large ranchos that eventually became the 240,000 acre San Simeon ranch. As a youth, Hearst traveled extensively with his mother Phoebe, seeing many of the world's cultural centers. This early exposure to the arts led to a passion for collecting. In college he was business manager for Harvard's Lampoon and after worked for Joseph Pulitzer. In 1887, Hearst took over the *San Francisco Examiner* from his father and launched his publishing empire of 26 newspapers, 16 magazines, 11 radio stations, 5 news services and 1 movie company. Hearst served as United States Senator from California and later as a United States Representative from New York.

The principle architect of the castle was Julia Morgan, one of the foremost architects in the country and a long-time collaborator with Hearst's mother. The two women first worked together on the architectural plan for the University of California at Berkeley. Construction of the castle began in 1919 and continued for 28 years until 1947, when illness forced Hearst to move to Los Angeles.

Courtesy of Hodgetts + Fung DAWN REHEARSAL IN NEW BOWL SHELL

HOLLYWOOD

Hollywood was a rural backwater in 1911 when the Nestor Film Company rented the old Blondeau Tavern and Barn on Sunset Blvd., launching a new chapter in California history. Producers were attracted to the town by the year-round warm weather and clear days, so good for shooting. The influx of entertainers and big money brought dozens of luxury hotels, nightclubs elegant restaurants, and theaters. Hollywood became the glamour capital of the world.

Perhaps the last remaining symbol of legendary Hollywood is **Grauman's Chinese Theater** on Hollywood Blvd. Sid Grauman opened the theater May 18, 1927, with Cecil B. deMille's *King of Kings*. Legend says he got the idea for the theater's famous Forecourt of the Stars when he saw Norma Talmadge accidentally step in wet cement opening night. Talmadge, Mary Pickford and Douglas Fairbanks, Sr. were the first entertainers to leave their impression, in 1927. Since then more than 180 stars have pressed their hands, feet, and signatures into the theater's courtyard.

The **Hollywood Bowl** (1922), is a natural amphitheater formed in the foothills above Hollywood. A museum there features changing exhibits of rare musical instruments.

Nearby, the **Hollywood Heritage Museum** displays early filmmaking equipment and memorabilia. It is housed in the barn used by deMille in the film *The Straw Man*.

The **Walk of Fame** begins at Hollywood Blvd. and Highland Ave. where the first stars were placed in 1960. Thousands of stars have since been added, extending down the boulevard to Hollywood and Vine.

While not technically part of Hollywood, the **Casino Building** on Santa Catalina Island is a part of Hollywood history. The Island originally served as a hideout for pirates and smuggling operations. In the 1920s it became a favorite "get-away" for Hollywood entertainers. The historic, 12-story Art Deco rotunda, the first completely circular structure in modern times, was built in 1929. Inside, the Avalon Theater was the first to be designed for sound movies. The great directors of Hollywood often premiered their epics here to friends, followed by grand soirees in the lavish Casino Ballroom. At 180 feet in diameter with no interior columns, it is the largest such ballroom in the world.

Los Angeles

El Pueblo de la Reina de Los Angeles al margen del Rio de la Porciuncula (City of the Queen of the Angeles by the bank of the Porciuncula River) was founded on September 4, 1781. The **Pueblo de Los Angeles State Historic Park** encompasses the plaza and surrounding buildings that were the origins of Los Angeles. The plaza was laid out in 1815 during the construction of the **Plaza Church**. The church was not part of the mission chain but rather a parish church built by the Franciscans to serve the families of the pueblo. The church has operated continuously since 1822.

The *rancheros* built their townhouses around the plaza, which was used for social gatherings and occasional bullfights. **Avila Adobe**, built for mayor Francisco Avila in 1818, is the oldest residence in Los Angeles. The home has been restored to its original appearance, including traditional Mexican furnishings. The Victorian-style **Sepulveda House** (1887) was a residence, hotel, and boarding house owned and operated by Eloisa Martinez de Sepulveda. The homes are restored with artifacts depicting the lifestyles of 19th-century Los Angeles.

The city's first firehouse, **Firehouse #1** (1884), is now a small museum displaying original firefighting equipment from the 1880's. Restaurants and shops occupy other historic buildings. **Olvera Street**, the oldest in the city, has been converted into a Mexican open-air market.

Metrolink LOS ANGELES UNION STATION

The downtown area's historic sites include the 1920's Art Deco **Union Station**, and **Grand Central Market** (1917), offering an extensive variety of ethnic foods and open market stalls. The market is located in the first fireproof building in Los Angeles, built in 1897 by Homer Laughlin.

Adjacent to the University of Southern California is Exposition Park, home to the L.A. Coliseum, a beautiful seven-acre rose garden, and three museums. **The Natural History Museum of Los Angeles County**, established in 1913, is the largest on the west coast and the third largest in the country. It is unique in that it includes American Pioneer History along with natural science exhibits featuring California ecology, gems, and minerals, African and North American pre-Historic mammals, and Pre- Columbian art and artifacts from the ancient Maya, Aztec, and Inca civilizations. The exhibit on gold features some of the World's finest specimens displayed in a simulated gold mine. A **Children's Discovery Center** within the museum is full of interactive exhibits.

Many visitors have difficulty getting past the Science Court entrance attractions of **The California Science Center.** In the Center itself, fun and informative interactive exhibits focus on: human inventions and innovations; flying and exploring the stars; and life form connections. Also featured are fantastic special exhibits that change frequently, so try to visit often. Another feature in historic Exposition Park is the **California Afro-American Museum** offering exhibits of traditional, modern and contemporary art of Afro-Americans.

Hancock Park on Wilshire Blvd. contains two of the city's leading museums, as well as the **La Brea Tar Pits**, the world's foremost deposit of Ice Age fossils. This Pleistocene meadow contains millions of fossils, dating back 40,000 years, of animals trapped in a natural asphalt pit. It is the largest such collection ever found. Europeans first noted the pits during the Portola expedition of 1769, although Native Americans had used the natural asphalt for centuries. In fact, the asphalt was deemed so important to pueblo life that the Mexican Government provided for public access and use of the pits as part of the land grant of El Rancho La Brea. Fossils were first discovered in 1875, and the land given to the state for excavation in 1913 by Allan Hancock. In 1975, George C. Page began construction of a museum, which includes some fun exhibits for children. Fossils of saber-toothed cats, wooly mammoths, mastodons, and a young woman who lived 9,000 years ago during the Ice Age are displayed at the **Page Museum at the La Brea Tar Pits**, a satellite of the Natural History Museum of Los Angeles County.

Peter Brenner

PAVILION FOR JAPANESE ART

The Los Angeles County Museum of Art is one of the largest in the country, containing artworks dating from prehistoric to present times. Three buildings house exhibits of Asian, Indian, and Islamic art, pre-Columbian costumes and textiles, a collection of glass spanning from Roman to Victorian times, European painting from the Medieval through the Modern periods, 20th-century sculpture, and American arts and crafts. **The Pavilion for Japanese Art**, built specifically for the museum's extensive Asian collections, was designed by Bruce Goff and Bart Prince using a translucent material for the walls and ceiling to produce the subdued lighting effect created by paper walls in traditional Japanese homes. The movement of the clouds and sun became part of the works, as was intended by the artists. Included are over 300 screen and scroll paintings from the renowned Shin'enkan collection.

The **Museum of Contemporary Art** has three separate branches, two downtown Los Angeles and a third in West Hollywood. It is the only museum in Los Angeles devoted exclusively to post-World War II art, and presents a variety of media including environmental pieces, dance, and video.

Jack Ross J. PAUL GETTY MUSEUM

Reputed to be the richest museum in the world, the **J. Paul Getty Museum** in Malibu houses an outstanding collection of the world's masterpieces. Getty began collecting art in the 1930s. The main collection reflects his interest in Greek ànd Roman antiquities, Renaissance and Baroque paintings, and European decorative arts. Illuminated manuscripts from the 9th through the 17th centuries, drawings, sculptures, and photographs have been added. Leonardo, Rubens, Ingres, Cézanne, Rembrandt, Gainsborogh, David, van Gogh, Munch, Gaimbologna, and de Vries are just a few of the renowned artists represented.

Even the museum is a work of art. The grounds are lush with waterfalls, flowering shrubs, and palm trees in the manor of Roman landscaping. The main building is a recreation of an ancient Roman estate modeled after the Villa dei Papiri near Naples. The original villa was buried by the volcanic eruption near Pompeii in AD 79. Getty bought the estate in the 1940s, and in 1971 the museum was commissioned. It is free and accessible by bus, but parking reservations are necessary.

The **Southwest Museum**, L.A.'s first museum, contains one of the most outstanding collections for Native American art and artifacts in the U.S. The museum was founded in 1907 by Charles Fletcher Lummis, a journalist and

Lawrence Reynolds NAVAJO BLANKETS, SOUTHWEST MUSEUM

archeologist, and includes pre-historic through modern art by Southwest, Great Plains, Northwest Coast and California tribes. Among the artifacts are basketry, pottery, textiles, and ornamental objects and clothing. The museum also operates the **Casa de Adobe**, a recreation of a pre-1850 Mexican rancho which exhibits Latino art and artifacts.

Skirball Cultural Center and Museum links Jewish American life and democratic values through exhibits and programs for all backgrounds. The Children's Discovery Center has wonderful hands-on archeology exhibits.

Fans of the Old West will enjoy the **Museum of the American West**, which presents the history and culture of the American West through paintings by noted Western artists such as Frederic Remington. There are also exhibits of clothing, tools, toys, antique firearms, Western films and documentaries, and a 19th-century fire engine. The museum is located at Griffith Park, along with the **Los Angeles Zoo**, **Griffith Observatory and Planetarium**, and **Travel Town**, an outdoor museum of steam trains, wagons and early automobiles. A miniature 1880s steam train takes children on rides through the park.

Los Angeles County has several interesting residence museums. The Los Angeles County Arboretum in Arcadia features the **Hugo Reid Adobe** (1839), Lucky Baldwin's **Queen Anne Cottage** (1879), and the **Santa Anita Depot** (1890), built by the Sante Fe Railroad and outfitted with original furnishings. In Long Beach, the **General Phineas Banning Residence Museum** is one of the state's finest examples of Greek Revival architecture. The home was built in 1864 for a prominent railroad and shipping baron and is surrounded by Banning Park. **Will Rogers State Historic Park** in Pacific Palisades preserves the humorist's home and memorabilia, and includes picnic areas, horse and hiking trails.

MONTEREY STATE BEACH

MONTEREY

Monterey is probably California's most historically significant city. Until 1850, it was the social and political center of California. The Monterey Historical Society has splendidly preserved the city's historic sites. **The Path of History Walking Tour** includes numerous homes and public buildings, many open to the public. A self-guided tour starts at Fisherman's Wharf.

The peninsula was first inhabited by the Ohlone Indians. Explorer Sebastian Vizcaino raised the Spanish flag at what is now **Custom Plaza** in 1602, naming the peninsula for Count de Monte Rey, the viceroy of New Spain. In 1770, Captain Gaspar de Portola established **El Real Presidio de Monterey**, while Father Serra founded the state's second mission. In 1775, Monterey was made capital of California and remained so through the Spanish and Mexican periods.

Monterey Bay is one of the few safe harbors on the California coast, which accounts for its prominence. It became the center of trading activity in the early 1800s when Mexico established a customs house here in 1822 to collect duties on foreign trade. The original **Customs House** is still standing. Inside is an example of a typical ship's cargo of the 1830's: porcelain from China, rum from Bermuda, cartwheels from New England, grain, cloth, and household goods from around the world. In 1846 the building was expanded to its present size. Occasionally, it was used for banquets and public festivities. It was at the Customs House U.S. Naval Commodore John Drake Sloat raised the American flag on July 7th, 1846, thus extending American territory "from sea to shining sea."

American military commanders continued to govern the territory from Monterey, and the city remained the center of political and governmental activity until 1850, when San Jose was named capital of the newly formed state. The state constitution was written and signed in Monterey at **Colton Hall**, a schoolhouse and public facility built in 1848 by the city's first American alcalde, Walter Colton.

Monterey is the only city in the U. S. to have headquartered an American embassy to a foreign country. In 1843, Thomas Larkin, a prominent businessman, was made U. S. Consul to California. **Larkin House**, a two-story adobe on Calle Principal, served as a political center. It is typical of Monterey's Colonial-style homes. Another historic residence is the **Cooper-Molera Complex**, home of John Rogers Cooper, Larkin's half-brother, and Cooper's wife Encarnacion Vallejo, sister of General Mariano Guadalupe Vallejo. The large two-story adobe residence, Cooper's store, and various business and residential buildings are an outstanding example of Mexican-era architecture in Monterey. Capt. Cooper imported home furnishings from China, Mexico, and New England, which are on display. The home has been meticulously restored and provides a glimpse into the lifestyle enjoyed by Monterey's elite.

The town's only remaining Spanish structure is the **Royal Presidio Chapel**. The original mission, founded by Father Serra in 1770, was moved to Carmel and an adobe chapel was built to serve the *presidio*. It has been in continuous use

Stanton Center FRESNEL LENS

since 1795. Most of the main structure, the front facade, the stations of the cross, and many other features are original. The bas-relief of the Virgin of Guadalupe, Mexico's patron saint, high up on the front facade, was carved by Manuel Ruiz in 1791.

Across the Customs House Plaza is the new **Maritime Museum of Monterey at Stanton Center**. Its large collection includes nautical instruments and cultural memorabilia reflecting the history of Monterey, Here are more than 130 model ships, plus nautical paintings, documents, photographs, lithographs, and research materials, Additional exhibits focus on flags, charts and navigation, commerce, fishing, and lighthouses. In the lobby is a precision-crafted 16-foot Fresnel Lens (1889) from the old Point Sur lighthouse. Its light could be seen 24 miles offshore.

In nearby **Cannery Row**, the **Monterey Bay Aquarium** lets travelers explore the bay's marine life. The facilities focus entirely on Monterey Bay's unique eco-system. The bay is as large as the Grand Canyon and supports all levels of the food chain, from sardines to whales, giant squid, and great white sharks. The aquarium is built on what was once a sardine canning wharf in the heart of **Cannery Row**, made famous by John Steinbeck. The old canneries that once packed more than 240,000 tons of sardines annually now house shops, clubs, and restaurants.

SAN JUAN BAUTISTA S.H.P.

Other historic sites in the area include **San Juan Bautista State Historic Park** near Salinas. Many historic buildings have been preserved, and on the first Saturday of each month park rangers dress in period costumes for Living History Day to recreate life in the 1860s. In Salinas is the **Boronda Adobe** (c. 1844) and the **Steinbeck House**. In Carmel is the original **Mission San Carlos Borromeo** (1770) and **Tor House**, built of stones by poet Robinson Jeffers in the early 1900s.

ORANGE COUNTY

Orange County is known for its coastal resorts and amusement parks. **Knott's Berry Farm** is the oldest theme park in the country. It began in the 1930s with a few kiddie rides and entertainment for families waiting for a table at Mrs. Knott's famed fried chicken restaurant. The 160 acre theme park features a wide variety of attractions for all ages. Knott's Ghost Town has been assembled with authentic buildings brought from mining towns throughout the West.

G.R. Fessler MAIN ENTRANCE FANTASYLAND

Anaheim is home for **Disneyland Park** and **Disney's California Adventure Park**. In 1955, Walt Disney created "the happiest place on earth" and more magic has been created with the addition of the California Adventure Park. These parks are a destination for visitors from around the world. Schedule your visit as far in advance as possible.

In Santa Anna, **The Bowers Museum of Cultural Art**, founded in 1932 presents the fine art of indigenous peoples from around the world. Pre-Columbian, native American, African, and Oceanic cultures are represented in both ancient and modern pieces.

Laguna Beach began as an artists' colony, as evidenced by the abundance of galleries. The city sponsors a unique

Pageant of the Masters re-creation of Leonardo's LAST SUPPER

artistic event each summer, **The Laguna Beach Festival of Arts and Pageant of the Masters**. Since 1933, local artists have gathered to create tableaux of famous paintings and artworks, set to music. Spectators enjoy life-sized renditions of Seurat, Leonardo, Erté and others. The first paintings performed were *Mona Lisa, Whistler's Mother*, and *Blue Boy*. Today, hundreds of volunteers are involved making costumes, creating sets, and posing motionless in the productions. The pageant, started by John Hinchman to attract visitors to the artists' colony, now attracts international attention as the best tableau vivant event in the world. **The Laguna Art Museum** is widely acclaimed for its exhibits of California Impressionists.

Traveling down the coast, Dana Point harbors a full-sized replica of **The Pilgrim**, a trading brig made famous by Richard Henry Dana in his book *Two Years Before the Mast*. Dana was a Harvard student who turned to sailing in hopes of healing his poor eyesight. In 1834 he traveled to California and wrote in fascinating detail about the land, the people, and the experience. This small, picturesque cove was a favorite of his and thus bears his name.

Further south is San Juan Capistrano, best known for the swallows that return each year to the mission on St. Joseph's Day, March 19, and depart on October 23. **The Serra Chapel** is the oldest building in the state, dating from 1778. The city maintains its historic atmosphere by preserving many lovely adobe homes. In Yorba Linda, the **Richard M. Nixon Library & Birthplace** is a popular attraction. The nine-acre site includes a museum gallery, archives and reference library.

PASADENA

Pasadena, home to the famous Tournament of Roses Parade, was founded in 1874 by a group of Midwesterners seeking refuge from cold winter weather. They built a city of fine public buildings, elegant homes, tree-lined streets, and Victorian rose gardens. Pasadena has converted many historic buildings into nationally renowned museums. The Pasadena Historical Society is housed in **Fenyes Mansion** (1905). Its original furnishings and artworks depict turn-of-the-century Pasadena. Also displayed is a collection of Finnish folk art. The society publishes a guide to Pasadena's best preserved houses and architectural styles.

Huntington Library THE LIBRARY BUILDINC

The Huntington Library, Art Collections, and Botanical Gardens (1919) houses the collections of railroad and real estate magnate Henry E. Huntington. The library displays one of the world's finest collections of rare books and manuscripts. Included are a Gutenberg Bible printed on vellum, a manuscript of Chaucer's *Canterbury Tales*, the double-elephant folio edition of Audubon's *Birds of America*, Benjamin Franklin's handwritten autobiography, and the world's foremost collection of first edition folios by William Shakespeare.

Housed in what was the main residence, the **Huntington Art Collections** contains an outstanding collection of 17th and 18th century British and French art. Important works by Gainsborough, Watteau, Boucher, and Fragonard are on display. The Virginia Steele Scott Gallery specializes in

American paintings from the 1730s to 1930s, while the Arabella Huntington Collection features Renaissance painting and 18th century French sculpture, tapestries, and furnishings.

The Botanical Gardens cover 130 acres of the estate with 13 distinct gardens. Most acclaimed is the Desert Garden, the largest mature cacti garden in the United States. The Rose Garden tells the history of roses over the past 2,000 years.

The Pacific Asia Museum introduced Pacific and Asian cultures to southern California. In 1970, its exhibits and demonstrations were moved to their permanent location in the **Grace Nicholson Building** (1929). Nicholson, a well-known Asian and Native American art collector in the 1920s, built her home and gallery in authentic Chinese Imperial Palace style. The building is now listed on the National Register of Historic Places. Its Courtyard Garden is one of only two authentic Chinese gardens in the United States. The museum hosts numerous cultural exchange programs and includes a contemporary Asian arts gallery, a student workshop, and a research library.

The Norton Simon Museum of Art features collections of Renaissance to mid-20th century European, Indian, and south Asian art. The museum houses works by renown artists such as van Gogh, Monet, Renoir, Matisse, and Picasso, as well as paintings and sculptures from India, Nepal, Kashmir, Thailand, and Cambodia, spanning a period of 2,500 years.

Among the fine homes in Pasadena, the **Gamble House** is internationally recognized as a masterpiece of the Arts and Crafts movement. Every aspect of the house was custom-designed: hand-rubbed fine woods, built-in cabinetry, multi-colored glass windows intended to create changing effects throughout the house. Even the lighting, furniture, and landscaping contribute to the whole. The house was built in 1908 by Greene & Greene, and is the best preserved example of the firm's Craftsman architecture.

Many private and public buildings have been registered as National or State Historic Landmarks. **The Pasadena Playhouse** (1917) and **El Alisal,** the 1898 Craftsman home of Charles Fletcher Lummis are but two examples. El Alisal, houses the Historical Society of Southern California. **Tournament House and Wrigley Gardens** (1914), built by William Wrigley of chewing gum fame, is headquarters for the Tournament of Roses Parade. The surrounding rose garden is open to the public. **Heritage Square** is a village of restored Victorian buildings recreating the atmosphere of southern California between 1865 and 1914.

Turtle Bay Exploration Park SUNDIAL BRIDGE

Redding

Northern California is a mountainous region originally settled by trappers and gold miners. In its largest city, Redding, are the **Turtle Bay Museums and Arboretum on the River,** a merger of Carter House Natural Science Museum, Redding Arboretum by the River, the Forest Museum and the Redding Museum of Art & History. Turtle Bay is a cultural and scientific center with a focus on the Sacramento River watershed. The focus is on the connections between people and nature in order to explore the challenges created by human use of the natural and cultural environment. The 300-acre Turtle Bay campus, situated on both sides of the Sacramento River, is joined by a spectacular 700-foot glass-deck pedestrian bridge.

West of Redding, in Shasta City, **Shasta State Historic Park**, is a monument to the gold-rush days. The restored courthouse operates as a museum. South of Redding, in Red Bluff, the **William B. Ide Adobe SHP** remembers California's only president. In June 1846, Ide joined a small group of trappers and homesteaders in a rebellion against the Mexican government in what became known as the Bear Flag Revolt. California's independence lasted a mere 25 days, when the new republic became a U. S. territory. His home on the Sacramento River depicts the life of California's pioneer families.

Bidwell Mansion SHP in Chico was built by Congressman John Bidwell in the 1880s. The 26-room Victorian Italianate-style home was visited by many civic leaders of the time. The mansion was built on the grounds of Rancho del Arroyo Chico, Bidwell's 22,000 acre ranch.

The mining town of Paradise is home to the **Gold Nugget Museum**, featuring a miner's cabin, blacksmith shop and general store, and a replica of a gold mine. In Weaverville, the **Joss House SHP** has an 1873 Chinese temple, fully restored to its original condition. The town of Yreka, established in 1851, boasts a nationally registered historic district of well-maintained Victorian-era homes, some of which are now bed-and-breakfast inns.

CALIFORNIA MUSEUM OF PHOTOGRAPHY

RIVERSIDE

Riverside was once the economic center of southern California, thanks to a "gold rush' of sorts. As an experiment, Eliza Tibbets planted two Brazilian navel orange trees in 1873. From them, the famed California citrus industry was born. By 1895, Riverside had become the wealthiest city per capita in the nation.

Evidence of the city's early wealth is apparent in its fine public buildings. The **Riverside Municipal Museum** is housed in a 1912 Classic Revival-style building and showcases Indian artifacts and natural science exhibits. Several elaborate Victorian homes have been fully restored and the Queen Anne-style **Heritage House** is open for tours. The house is considered the finest example of Victorian renovation in the state.

The historic **Mission Inn Hotel** is a National Landmark. Nearby **The California Museum of Photography** presents antique cameras and equipment, early daguerreotypes, and contemporary prints by leading photographers. Many cameras date back to the earliest days of photography. This is one of the most extensive collections in the country. The architecture of the building is distinctive. The lobby replicates a camera lens, projecting the outside world on the walls inside — upside-down as they occur inside a camera. Visitors are encouraged to learn about photography at the Interactive Gallery, through such activities as making a motion picture using an antique zoatrope.

The **Riverside Art Museum** occupies the former YWCA building (1929) designed by Julia Morgen. Morgen is best known for her collaboration with W. R. Hearst on Hearst's castle at San Simeon.

In south Riverside County, the **Temecula Valley Museum** chronicles the area's Luiseño Indians along with the influences of Mission San Rey, stagecoaches and the railroad.

DELTA KING, OLD TOWN SACRAMENTO

Sacramento

Sacramento's history began in 1839 when Captain John Sutter, a Swiss immigrant, built a fort at the confluence of the American and Sacramento Rivers. **Sutter's Fort** has been restored and is now a state historic park. Adjacent to the fort is the **State Indian Museum**, which displays California Indian art and artifacts.

When gold was discovered on Sutter's property, thousands of prospectors from around the world headed for the hills, often arriving by boat in San Francisco. The Forty-niners, as they were called, took paddle boats from San Francisco to Sacramento, where they headed overland to the Mother Lode. Sacramento quickly grew into a rowdy, riverside boom town.

Much of the city's original business district along the Sacramento River has been preserved in **Old Sacramento**. Wooden sidewalks, cobblestone streets, shops and restaurants recall the days of Black Bart and the Pony Express. The history exhibits of **Discovery Museum** housed in a reconstruction of the 1864 City Hall and waterworks trace the capital city's development.

In 1860, William Russell organized The Pony Express "to provide weekly mail delivery between St. Joseph, Missouri, and Sacramento". It was a dangerous job for which riders were paid $100 a month. Delivery costs were $5 per half ounce. Nevertheless, the Pony Express became widely used because of its dependability. When government postal costs reached as much as $135 a letter, Congress developed alternative means of correspondence, namely the wire service and transcontinental railways. **The B. F. Hastings Building** in Old Sacramento, originally the western terminus of the Pony Express, now contains exhibits on the celebrated delivery service in the **Wells Fargo Museum**.

Because of the Gold Rush, Sacramento became a major transportation center. The transcontinental railroad was completed in 1869, financed in part by Sacramento entrepreneurs Collis P. Huntington, Mark Hopkins, Charles Crocker, and Leland Stanford. **The California State Railroad Museum** in Old Sacramento has 21 completely restored locomotives, including the world's largest steam engine, and dozens of railroad artifacts.

Dept. of Parks & Recreation STATE CAPITOL

The **California State Capitol** is an impressive building of marble and granite, its classic Roman-Corinthian columns rising 210-feet to a gold-covered cupola. Begun in 1860, it took 14 years to complete. The ornate Victorian interior is equally impressive, with magnificent floor mosaics of marble and tile, artworks, decorative friezes, mahogany staircases and crystal chandeliers. The building underwent a massive restoration (1975-1982) that returned it to its original splendor. Seven historic period rooms, researched and appointed with more than 10,000 original antiques, are open to the public; free guided tours are offered. **The Governor's Mansion** is also open to the public.

The oldest public art museum in the state is the **Crocker Art Museum**, founded in 1873. The **Towe Auto Museum** operated by the California Vehicle Federation houses an extensive array of vintage automobiles. The collection of Fords is the most complete, but most other manufacturers are represented.

SAN DIEGO

Cabrillo National Monument on Point Loma marks the spot where Portuguese explorer Juan Rodriguez Cabrillo arrived in 1542 to claim this area for Spain. Nearly 250 years later, San Diego became the first European settlement in Alta ("Upper") California, when in1769 Padre Serra and Captain de Portola established the first mission and fortified settlement **Mission San Diego de Alcala.** Today the Mission still serves as an active parish church as well as an historic site. In 1774, the mission was moved from Presidio Hill to its present location in Mission Valley. The **Junipero Serra Museum** is now on Presidio Hill, a 40-acre landscaped park overlooking the Pacific Ocean and Mission Bay.

California State Parks

Nearby is **Old Town San Diego SHP**, which contains numerous historic buildings carefully restored to their original condition. Portions of the original mission and Presidio, along with restaurants, shops, and galleries, are in the area. Old Town represents the Mexican and Early American periods between 1821 and 1869.

The Gaslamp Quarter, originally known as New Town, has been designated a National Historic District. New Town was developed in 1857 as an effort to create a city center along the waterfront. Galleries, antique shops, and restaurants now occupy the restored Victorian buildings. Along the nearby waterfront is the **Maritime Museum**, housing the steam powered ferry, *Berkeley*, and the 1863 sailing ship *Star of India*. Further along the wharf is the **San Diego Aircraft Carrier Museum**, home to the legendary carrier **Midway** and its hangar of meticulously restored vintage aircraft.

One of the most beautiful urban parks in the country is **Balboa Park**, landscaped with exotic plants and native California trees and shrubbery. It was developed for the 1915-16 Panama-California Exposition. Many of the Moorish and Spanish-renaissance style buildings have been restored to house more than a dozen museums and exhibits. The **San Diego Zoo**, occupying the northwest corner of the park, is one of the largest in the world. Nearly 4,000 animals roam in recreations of their native habitats. Balboa Park projects a turn-of-the-century atmosphere with free concerts on one of the world's largest outdoor organs, a 1910 Herschell-Spillman carousel, a miniature railroad ride for the kids and lawn bowling. Tram rides from the parking areas deliver visitors to the many park attractions.

Within Balboa Park is the **San Diego Museum of Art**, known for its collection of Spanish art. Adjacent is the **Timken Museum of Art**, featuring a large collection of Russian icons. **The San Diego Museum of Man** traces the development of San Diego's earliest inhabitants from 5000-year-old Del Mar Man and 3000-year-old Kumeyaay Indians to the present. Also on El Prado is the **Natural History Museum**, the **Reuben H. Fleet Science Center** with an IMAX theater, and **Casa deBalboa**, a large Spanish renaissance style exhibition hall housing several small museums, including the **Model Railroad Museum**. On Pan American Plaza is the **Aerospace Museum** and the **San Diego Automotive Museum.**

Reminiscent of days past, the **Hotel del Coronado** is one of the last great resorts, built in the 1880s. The building has been designated a National Historic Landmark and is well worth a visit. From the grounds, travelers are rewarded with a lovely view of San Diego.

Scripps Institution of Oceanography SCRIPPS PIER

Located in La Jolla (*hoi-ya*) is the world-renown **Scripps Institution of Oceanography** and **Birch Aquarium**. The **Museum of Contemporary Art**, with locations downtown and in La Jolla, specializes in American and European art since the 1950s. On the seaward side of the museum in La Jolla is **Ellen Scripps Browning Park**, named for the philanthropist whose Irving Gill-designed home now houses the art museum.

At the **Palomar Observatory and Museum**, located on Palomar Mountain in northern San Diego county, visitors can look through a telescope at quasars, asteroids and distant galaxies. Photographs of the Observatory's discoveries are displayed in a small lobby museum.

CALIFORNIA HISTORIC SITES AND MUSEUMS
0 40 80 Miles
0 40 80 Kilometers
14 Number refers to page in book
31 East Bay
Univ. Of California
Oakland Mus.
Behring Auto Mus.
U.C. Berkeley Mus. of Art, Science & Culture
John Muir N.H.S.
26 San Francisco
San Francisco Cable Cars
Cable Car Museum
Fisherman's Wharf
S.F. National Maritime Mus.
Golden Gate N.R.A.
Alcatraz Island
Fort Mason
S.F. Presidio
Presidio Army Museum
Golden Gate Bridge
Wells Fargo History Mus.
Chinatown
Chinese Cult. Center
Old St. Mary's Church
Golden Gate Park
Conservatory of Flowers
Strybing Arboretum & Botanical Gardens
Japanese Tea Gardens
M.H. de Young Mem. Mus.
Palace of the Legion of Honor
Asian Art Museum
Steinhart Aquarium
Museum of National History
Morrison Planetarium
Palace of Fine Arts
S.F. Museum of Modern Art
Mission Dolores
37 Napa Valley
Mission San Francisco Solano
Jack London S.H.P.
Toscano Hotel
Depot Park Museum
Buena Vista Winery
Petaluma Adobe S.H.P.
Sonoma Barracks
Silverado Museum
36 Santa Cruz
Santa Cruz Beach Boardwalk
The Giant Dipper
Looff Carousel
Cocoanut Grove Casino
Walking Tour
Roaring Camp & Big Trees RR
11 Monterey
Path of History
Custom Plaza
El Real Presidio
Colton Hall
Larkin House
Cooper-Molera Complex
Royal Presidio Chapel
Maritime Museum
Cannery Row
Monterey Bay Aquarium
San Juan Bautista S.H.P.
Boronda Adobe
Steinbeck House
San Carlos Borromeo
Tor House
34 Santa Barbara
El Presidio S.H.P.
El Cuartel
Red Tile Tour
Historical Museum
County Courthouse/ Sunken Gardens
Mission Santa Barbara
Mus. of Natural Hist.
Botanical Gardens
Museum of Art
Little Red Schoolhouse
Matteis Tavern
Cold Springs Tavern
Carriage Museum
14 Orange County
Knott's Berry Farm
Disneyland
Movieland Wax Mus.
Hobby City Doll & Toy Museum
Bowers Museum of Cultural Art
Laguna Beach Festival of the Arts
Laguna Art Museum
The Pilgrim
Serra Chapel
Hearst San Simeon S.H.M.
PACIFIC OCEAN
OREGON
NEVADA
CALIFORNIA
Medford
Ashland
Klamath Falls
Lakeview
Brookings
Crescent City
Klamath
Orick
Arcata
Eureka
Fortuna
Yreka
Weed
Mount Shasta
Tulelake
LAVA BEDS NATL. MON.
Alturas
Canby
Adin
Bieber
Shasta Lake
Redding
Anderson
Weaverville
WHISKEYTOWN-SHASTA-TRINITY NATL. REC. AREA
Susanville
Westwood
Red Bluff
Corning
Orland
Willows
Chico
Paradise
Oroville
Quincy
Portola
Sparks
Reno
Truckee
Grass Valley
Gridley
Marysville
Yuba City
South Lake Tahoe
Auburn
Woodland
Citrus Heights
Sacramento
Garberville
KING RANGE NAT. CONS. AREA
Leggett
Fort Bragg
Mendocino
Willits
Ukiah
Lakeport
Clear Lake
Point Arena
Cloverdale
Healdsburg
Santa Rosa
Petaluma
POINT REYES NATL. SEASHORE
Napa
Fairfield
Lodi
Stockton
Manteca
Jackson
San Andreas
Sonora
San Rafael
Berkeley
Oakland
San Francisco
San Mateo
Fremont
Tracy
San Jose
Sunnyvale
Turlock
Merced
Mariposa
Chowchilla
Madera
Santa Cruz
Watsonville
Monterey Bay
Gilroy
Hollister
Marina
Monterey
Salinas
Carmel
PINNACLES NATL. MON.
Soledad
Greenfield
Big Sur
King City
Coalinga
Mendota
Selma
Hanford
Avenal
San Simeon
Cambria
Paso Robles
Atascadero
San Luis Obispo
Pismo Beach
Santa Maria
Lompoc
Santa Barbara
Santa Miguel Island
Santa Rosa Island
San Nicolas Island

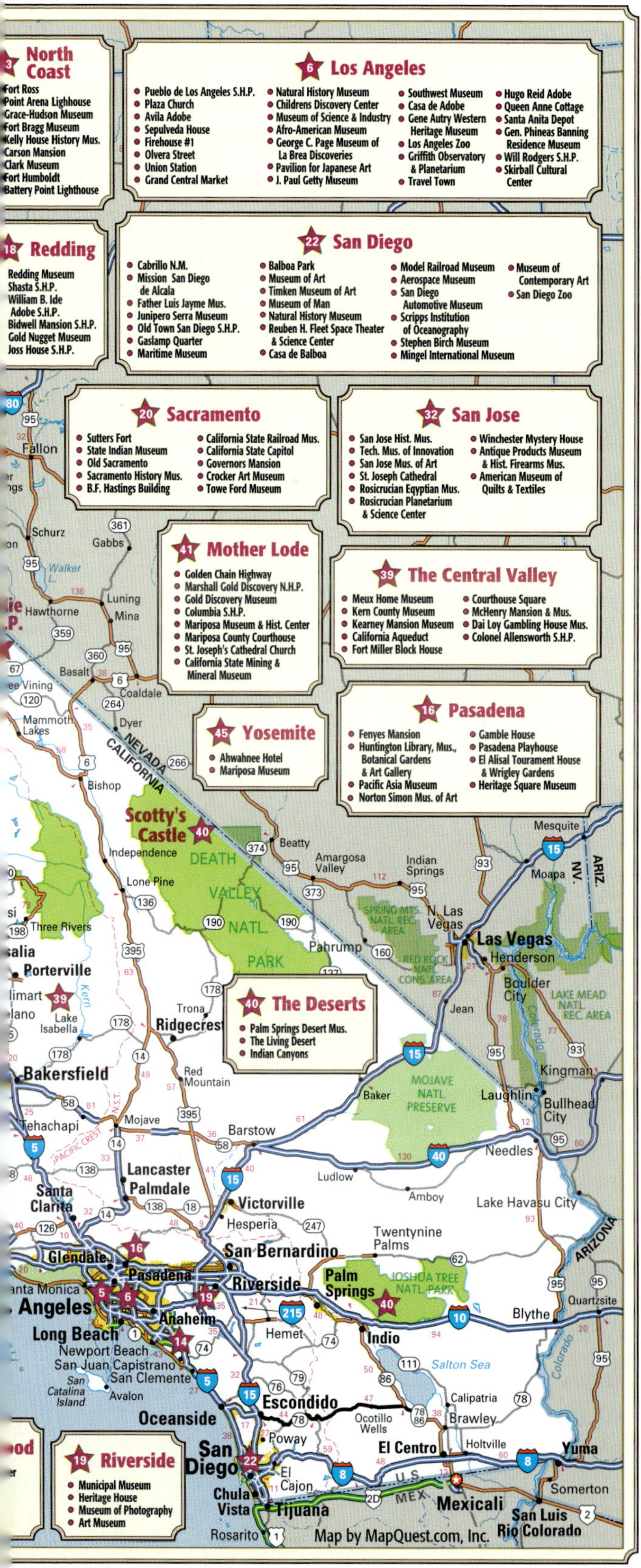
3 North Coast
Fort Ross
Point Arena Lighthouse
Grace-Hudson Museum
Fort Bragg Museum
Kelly House History Mus.
Carson Mansion
Clark Museum
Fort Humboldt
Battery Point Lighthouse
6 Los Angeles
Pueblo de Los Angeles S.H.P.
Plaza Church
Avila Adobe
Sepulveda House
Firehouse #1
Olvera Street
Union Station
Grand Central Market
Natural History Museum
Childrens Discovery Center
Museum of Science & Industry
Afro-American Museum
George C. Page Museum of La Brea Discoveries
Pavilion for Japanese Art
J. Paul Getty Museum
Southwest Museum
Casa de Adobe
Gene Autry Western Heritage Museum
Los Angeles Zoo
Griffith Observatory & Planetarium
Travel Town
Hugo Reid Adobe
Queen Anne Cottage
Santa Anita Depot
Gen. Phineas Banning Residence Museum
Will Rodgers S.H.P.
Skirball Cultural Center
18 Redding
Redding Museum
Shasta S.H.P.
William B. Ide Adobe S.H.P.
Bidwell Mansion S.H.P.
Gold Nugget Museum
Joss House S.H.P.
22 San Diego
Cabrillo N.M.
Mission San Diego de Alcala
Father Luis Jayme Mus.
Junipero Serra Museum
Old Town San Diego S.H.P.
Gaslamp Quarter
Maritime Museum
Balboa Park
Museum of Art
Timken Museum of Art
Museum of Man
Natural History Museum
Reuben H. Fleet Space Theater & Science Center
Casa de Balboa
Model Railroad Museum
Aerospace Museum
San Diego Automotive Museum
Scripps Institution of Oceanography
Stephen Birch Museum
Mingel International Museum
Museum of Contemporary Art
San Diego Zoo
20 Sacramento
Sutters Fort
State Indian Museum
Old Sacramento
Sacramento History Mus.
B.F. Hastings Building
California State Railroad Mus.
California State Capitol
Governors Mansion
Crocker Art Museum
Towe Ford Museum
32 San Jose
San Jose Hist. Mus.
Tech. Mus. of Innovation
San Jose Mus. of Art
St. Joseph Cathedral
Rosicrucian Eqyptian Mus.
Rosicrucian Planetarium & Science Center
Winchester Mystery House
Antique Products Museum & Hist. Firearms Mus.
American Museum of Quilts & Textiles
41 Mother Lode
Golden Chain Highway
Marshall Gold Discovery N.H.P.
Gold Discovery Museum
Columbia S.H.P.
Mariposa Museum & Hist. Center
Mariposa County Courthouse
St. Joseph's Cathedral Church
California State Mining & Mineral Museum
39 The Central Valley
Meux Home Museum
Kern County Museum
Kearney Mansion Museum
California Aqueduct
Fort Miller Block House
Courthouse Square
McHenry Mansion & Mus.
Dai Loy Gambling House Mus.
Colonel Allensworth S.H.P.
45 Yosemite
Ahwahnee Hotel
Mariposa Museum
16 Pasadena
Fenyes Mansion
Huntington Library, Mus., Botanical Gardens & Art Gallery
Pacific Asia Museum
Norton Simon Mus. of Art
Gamble House
Pasadena Playhouse
El Alisal Tourament House & Wrigley Gardens
Heritage Square Museum
Scotty's Castle 40
40 The Deserts
Palm Springs Desert Mus.
The Living Desert
Indian Canyons
19 Riverside
Municipal Museum
Heritage House
Museum of Photography
Art Museum
DEATH VALLEY NATL. PARK
MOJAVE NATL. PRESERVE
JOSHUA TREE NATL. PARK
LAKE MEAD NATL. REC. AREA
NEVADA
CALIFORNIA
ARIZONA
Las Vegas
Bakersfield
Los Angeles
San Bernardino
Riverside
Palm Springs
San Diego
Tijuana
Mexicali
Map by MapQuest.com, Inc.

CABLE CAR

San Francisco

There were fewer than 900 people living in San Francisco when gold was discovered in the Sierra foothills. With the ensuing gold rush, the population swelled to 40,000 by 1849. San Francisco soon acquired a lawless reputation as the western-most outpost of the Wild West. These origins may account for the strong dedication San Franciscans feel toward preserving the city's many cultural and historic sites.

Perhaps most famous are the **San Francisco Cable Cars**, the only National Historic Landmark on wheels. The cable cars were invented in 1873 by Andrew S. Hallidie to climb the city's exceedingly steep hills. This is the only operating cable car system in the world, and the most energy-efficient mass transit system in the country. The cable cars long served as the city's primary mode of transportation—in 1984 they were mechanically overhauled and restored to their original appearance. No trip to San Francisco is complete without a ride on the precarious Powell/Hyde Street line, around the 90-degree turns down Nob Hill to Fisherman's Wharf. The history and mechanics of the cable car system can be viewed at the **Cable Car Museum** at Washington and Mason streets.

The cable car tracks end at **Fisherman's Wharf**, just blocks away from the **San Francisco National Maritime Museum**. The museum operates five historic ships at Hyde Street Pier, along with the 1886 sailing ship *S/V Balclutha*. One of the country's finest collections of model ships, photos, and nautical artifacts recalls San Francisco's maritime history. The museum is part of **Golden Gate National Recreation Area**, the largest urban park in the country, with 72,000 acres of recreation.

Presidio Trust FORT SCOTT AT THE PRESIDIO OF SAN FRANCISCO

Other historic sites in the park are **Fort Mason**, and **Fort Point National Historic Site.** Fort Point, completed in 1861 to guard the channel, is typical of brick seacoast forts built by the Army Corps of Engineers at that time. Fort Point is on the grounds of the **San Francisco Presidio**, established in 1776, the Presidio served as a military installation under the flags of Spain (1776-1822), Mexico (1822-1848) and the United States (1848-1994). Today, the Presidio is a National Historic Landmark District of 1480 acres with 469 historic buildings constructed from the Civil War through World War II. The Park and Visitor Center are open year round.

Another popular attraction in the Golden Gate National Recreation Area is Alcatraz Island in San Francisco Bay. Views from the island are spectacular. Alcatraz was a maximum security federal penitentiary, known for housing notorious prisoners. Now open to the public, the 12 acre island is reached by ferry from Fisherman's Wharf. Schedule ahead for cellblock tours.

Few sites symbolize California like the **Golden Gate Bridge**. The Golden Gate, popularized when it became the

U.S. Geological Survey GOLDEN GATE BRIDGE

passageway to California's gold country, is the narrow channel between the Pacific Ocean and San Francisco Bay one of the world's most treacherous waterways. Powerful currents, rocky cliffs, and dense fog prevented early explorers from detecting the inlet by sea. Not until 1769 did Captain Gaspar de Portolá discover the bay on an overland expedition to Monterey. When engineers decided to span the channel, critics said it couldn't be done, but it was completed in 1937. Until 1964 it was the longest single-span suspension bridge ever built (4,200 feet). It's 746-foot towers support more than 100 million tons.

The California gold rush turned San Francisco from a sleepy outpost into the financial center of the West Coast. The nation's second mint was established here in 1852. As San Francisco continued to grow, the Mint was moved to larger facilities and in 1989 after an earthquake its minting operations were shut down. Located in the Financial District, the **Wells Fargo Museum** exhibits original Concord Stage Coaches and impressive collections of gold coins, telegraphs, gold nuggets and western fine art dating from the California Gold Rush Days to the present.

ENTRANCE TO CHINATOWN

Bustling sidewalks, hundred-year-old dragon pagoda-styled gas lamps, and open-air markets are a sure sign you're in **Chinatown.** In the 1800s Chinese laborers were recruited to work in the mines and later on the railroads. Ads in the Hong Kong newspapers promised high wages and opportunity in California. Today, Chinatown is one of the largest Chinese communities outside Asia. Old Chinatown Lane is two blocks down Washington Street from the Cable Car Museum The **Chinese Culture Center** presents the history of the district and the people. Within the district is **Old St. Mary's Church** (1854), a historical landmark located at Grant and California streets, and Jackson Square, an historic district that was the original Barbary Coast.

Clarence Towers, S.F. Rec. & Parks CONSERVATORY OF FLOWERS

Golden Gate Park is the result of some creative waste management. Manure recovered from the city's horse-drawn street cars was used to turn the city's netherlands into a lush urban park of gardens and museums, lakes, trails, and recreational areas. The oldest and loveliest building in the park is the elaborate Victorian **Conservatory of Flowers**. Crates of wrought iron and glass were shipped from England around Cape Horn, and construction was completed in 1879. The Conservatory houses a vast collection of tropical plants and orchids. **Strybing Arboretum and Botanical Gardens** covers 70 acres and hosts more than 6,000 plant species from around the world, earning it an international reputation. The **Japanese Tea Garden** is an authentic recreation of the gardens in Kyoto, created for the Midwinter International Exposition of 1894. The garden designed by Makoto Hagiwara, a widely-respected Japanese landscape architect who expanded the original exhibition garden to its present size, adding five acres of bonsai trees, stone lanterns, flowering cherry trees, pagodas, reflecting ponds, and teahouses.

The **M.H. de Young Memorial Museum** opened in March 1895 as a memorial to the California Midwinter International Exposition. De Young collected African, American and ancient art, which has become the core of the museum's permanent collection. The de Young houses one of the best collections of American painting in the country. Also included are Central and South American works and textiles, and outstanding examples of American craftsmanship.

The **Asian Art Museum of San Francisco** contains the largest collection of Asian art in the country. Across the Music Concourse is the **California Academy of Sciences**, containing the **Natural History Museum**, **Morrison Planetarium**, and **Steinhardt Aquarium**.

PALACE OF FINE ARTS

The **California Palace of the Legion of Honor** is in Lincoln Park, overlooking the Golden Gate Bridge. Containing some of the world's masterpieces, the collection includes decorative arts, sculpture, tapestries and paintings, dating back thousands of years. Special exhibitions are often featured and several hours should be allowed to view the collections.

Exploratorium is the city's acclaimed museum of science, art, and human perception. It was founded in 1969 by Dr. Frank Oppenheimer with the idea that the best way to learn about principles of nature is to experience them hands-on. More than 700 interactive exhibits let visitors translate their voices into color, make lightning from a radio wave, test reaction times, or paint with sun energy. The Exploratorium is in the **Palace of Fine Arts**, the last remaining building from the 1915 Pan-American Exposition.

San Francisco Museum of Modern Art first opened in 1935. The collection includes modern painting, photography, sculpture, media arts, architecture and design. The museum is located on Third Street in the South of Market district.

The city's oldest structure is **Mission San Francisco de Asis**, popularly called **Mission Dolores**, founded in 1776 by Father Junipero Serra. The chapel and museum are dwarfed by the adjoining basilica built in 1918, and is located at 16th Street and Dolores.

OAKLAND MUSEUM OF CALIFORNIA

EAST BAY

Oakland is well-known for its art deco buildings and hillside parklands. The **Oakland Museum of California** is devoted to the environment, history and art of California. The museum is an innovative three-tiered complex of gardens and galleries. This "architectural masterpiece" designed by Kevin Roche, John Diunkeloo and Associates, occupies four city blocks adjacent to Lake Meritt, near downtown Oakland. The terraced gardens are ideal for picnics and relaxing. Oakland's Zoo is nestled in the rolling hills of 525-acre Knowland Park. Over 300 native and exotic animals live in naturalistic habitats at the Zoo.

UC Berkeley is the oldest of the University of California's campuses and serves as the flagship of the state's public university system. Extensive libraries, museums and archives support research, teaching and public service.

In the small fishing village of Martinez is the **John Muir National Historic Site**, a Victorian mansion built by environmental activist John Muir in 1882. One of the founders

JOHN MUIR N.H.S.

of the Sierra Club, Muir encouraged the preservation of our nation's wilderness areas which helped establish the National Park Service.

Danville's **Eugene O'Neil National Historic Site** was home of the Nobel Prize-winning playwright. For car buffs, the **Blackhawk Auto Museum** in Danville exhibits over 100 unique automobiles.

ROSICRUCIAN EGYPTIAN MUSEUM

San Jose

The pueblo of San Jose, founded in 1777, was the first Spanish family settlement in California. The pueblo, situated in the fertile Santa Clara Valley at the southern end of San Francisco Bay, was intended to provide food for the soldiers stationed at the San Francisco and Monterey *presidios*. The city became the first capital of California and is today the third largest city in the state.

The **San Jose Historical Museum** has fully restored 21 buildings from turn-of-the-century San Jose. **Peralta Adobe**, the oldest remaining building from the Spanish period, dates from 1807. While paying homage to its historical roots, San Jose is a city looking to the future. The city's newest museum, The **Tech Museum of Innovation** in downtown San Jose provides educational experiences for children, families, and adults through exhibits and creative exploration. At the Tech, visitors can experiment with new technologies that predominate in surrounding Silicon Valley: robotics, semiconductors, space, and computer-aided design. The most popular exhibits are the robots, which perform household chores and other commands. Visitors can also design a hi-tech bicycle or take a simulated flight over Mars. The Tech is located near City Plaza Park, as is the **Children's Discovery Museum**. The museum, painted a child-pleasing purple, is a downtown landmark, inside, interactive exhibits invite kids to play, learn, and create their own works of art. The **San Jose Museum of Art** is housed in the city's 1897 Federal Building. Nearby is **St. Joseph Cathedral**, built in 1877.

The **Rosicrucian Egyptian Museum** grew out of the collection of Dr. H. Spencer Lewis in the early 1930s. In 1966, the collection moved into an Egyptian-styled building resembling the Karnak Temple of Anion at Thebes. It is the largest collection of Egyptian artifacts in the West, including numerous mummies and a reproduction of a walk-in rock tomb. Jewelry, pottery, and sculpture dating back 6,000 years are on display. The **Rosicrucian Planetarium** recounts the mythologies of ancient cultures as well as the newest scientific discoveries about the heavens.

WINCHESTER MYSTERY HOUSE

One of the more amazing sites in San Jose is the **Winchester Mystery House**, constructed by Sarah Winchester between 1884 and 1922. Mrs. Winchester became heiress to the Winchester Rifle fortune, estimated at $20 million, when her husband and daughter died unexpectedly in 1884. It is said she built her labyrinthine Victorian mansion to appease, or confuse, the angry spirits of persons killed by the famed "Gun that Won the West."

Mrs. Winchester continued construction around the clock for 38 years. There are secret passageways, chimneys that stop short of the ceiling, even a door that opens into the floor. Historians note "the house is so complex, even the owner and servants needed maps to find their way."

The house is beautifully constructed with elaborate hand-laid parquet floors, Tiffany glass, exquisite gold and silver chandeliers, fine furnishings, and the most modern conveniences of the time. A devout occultist, Mrs. Winchester probably would have been pleased that her mansion was designated a California Historical Landmark on Friday, May 13, 1974.

Also on the estate are the **Winchester Antique Products Museum** and the **Winchester Firearms Museum**. They feature antique rifles and a special collection of Limited Edition Winchester Commemorative Rifles, including the *Theodore Roosevelt* and the *John Wayne.*

The **San Jose Museum of Quilts and Textiles** displays fine antique quilts and modern textile art.

SANTA BARBARA COUNTY COURTHOUSE

SANTA BARBARA

When explorer Sebastian Vizcaino sought shelter in a large crescent shaped bayou December 4, 1602, Saint Barbara's Day, he named the landing site in her honor. With the construction of the royal presidio in 1782, the town became one of four major Spanish outposts in Alta California. At **El Presidio de Santa Barbara SHP** some of the original buildings remain, including **El Cuartel** (1788), the second oldest surviving structure in California. Other parts of the fort, such as the commandante's and padre's quarters, and Presidio Chapel, have been reconstructed with traditional adobe, a sun-dried brick made of mud and straw.

Architectural evidence of Santa Barbara's Spanish heritage is everywhere, especially in the distinctive whitewashed adobe and red tile roofs. New structures are built in harmony with the pre-existing style, giving the city a visual cohesiveness. Many of the city's older buildings and Spanish shopping arcades have been restored and stand side by side with newer structures. These buildings, prominent along State Street and the downtown area, are marked with glazed tiles which tell the history of the building. The **Red**

Tile Tour takes visitors by most of the city's historical buildings and several Mexican-era adobe residences belonging to some of the city's most prestigious families. Guides are available at information centers or at the **Santa Barbara Historical Museum**.

One of the most beautiful public buildings in California is the **Santa Barbara County Courthouse and Sunken Gardens**, built in 1929 and open for public tour. It is an impressive example of Spanish-Moorish architecture with turrets, balconies, and elaborate tile work. The clock tower provides an unbeatable 360-degree view of the city and the harbor.

Mission Santa Barbara is known as "Queen of the Missions" for its beautiful architecture and lovely gardens. Sailors trading on the coast once used the mission, easily visible in the foothills above the city as a landmark for anchoring offshore. Nearby is the **Museum of Natural History**. Farther up Mission Canyon Road is the **Santa Barbara Botanic Garden**, featuring 65 acres of native California trees, shrubs, and wildflowers.

S.B. Museum of Art APHRODITE

The Santa Barbara Museum of Art offers a widely-respected collection of works, from ancient Greek and Asian sculpture through contemporary art.

North of Santa Barbara are the Santa Ynez Mountains and the Santa Ynez Valley. In the valley, clustered in and around the town of Solvang, the *Danish Capital of America,* are the

Hans Christian Anderson Museum, operated by Solvang's Ugly Duckling Foundation; **Santa Ynez Valley Historical Society Museum** and **Parks Janeway Carriage House**. Part of the Historical Society museum, the Carriage House displays a fine collection of well-preserved horse-drawn vehicles. In Ballard, visit the historical **Little Red Schoolhouse**, it has been in continuous use since 1883.

Santa Cruz Seaside Co. THE GIANT DIPPER

SANTA CRUZ

Santa Cruz became popular as a spa and resort town in the 1860s when John Leibrandt set up a public bathhouse and encouraged visitors to "take the waters." **The Santa Cruz Beach Boardwalk** remains the only boardwalk and amusement park operating on the west coast and one of the few left in the world. The casino and boardwalk date from 1907 making it not only the last but the first West Coast boardwalk as well.

The main attraction is **The Giant Dipper**, repeatedly voted one of the world's great rollercoasters. Designer Arthur Looff set out to make a "combination earthquake, balloon ascension and aeroplane drop." The first drop is seven stories, and cars travel along 1/2-mile of track at 55 m.p.h. When the Dipper carried the first thrill seekers on May 17, 1924, rides cost 15 cents. Original construction cost was $50,000. Much less than a fresh coat of paint today.

The Boardwalk's **Looff Carousel** (1911) was created by Charles I. D. Looff, a Danish woodcarver renowned for his lively horses and chariots. The carousel has been fully restored, down to the brass rings. The original 342-pipe Ruth band organ, built in Germany in 1894, provides music for the ride. Both The Giant Dipper and The Looff Carousel are National Historic Landmarks.

The Cocoanut Grove Casino (1907), where big bands entertained WWII servicemen in the 1940s, hosts Sunday

Brunch and other special events, and offers a superb view of Monterey Bay. On the main floor, antique arcade games from the 1920s stand beside modern video games. **A Walking Tour** of the historic Santa Cruz Beach Boardwalk illuminates the resort's colorful history. In nearby Felton, the **Roaring Camp and Big Trees Railroad** takes travelers on an authentic 1880s narrow gauge steam train through thick groves of coastal redwoods.

SONOMA & NAPA

Sonoma was founded by Mexican General Mariano Guadalupe Vallejo, who laid out Sonoma Plaza in 1835. Surrounding the plaza are numerous historical buildings - Mexican adobes, western-style false-front buildings, and Italian basalt structures dating from the 1800s. Most notable of these are **Mission San Francisco Solano**, the **Sonoma Barracks**, and the **Toscano Hotel**. The hotel provides tours and the barracks house a small museum. The whole town center has been designated a National Historic District.

This quiet town was once a hotbed of rebellion. On June 14, 1846, a group of 24 rebels rode into town and declared California an independent republic. They elected William B. Ide president and, at Sonoma Plaza, raised the Bear Flag, crudely painted by Mary Todd Lincoln's nephew, William. It turned out to be a fairly harmless and unorganized group and the revolt was short lived. Just 25 days later on July 7, the Stars and Stripes were raised at the capital in Monterey, and California came under United States rule. The history of the California Republic is preserved at **The Depot Park Museum,** located in a replica of Sonoma's original train depot.

JACK LONDON S.H.P.

Several of the towns in Sonoma Valley have State Historic Parks. North of Sonoma is the **Jack London State Historic Park,** established in 1959 to preserve the estate of the world-famous author. California's largest adobe structure is the focus of the **Petaluma Adobe State Historic Park**. The rancho belonged to General Vallejo and served as a military headquarters from 1834 to 1846.

Franciscan monks began producing wine in the Napa/Sonoma region in the 1780s. However, the beginning of California's commercial wine industry is credited to Count Agoston Haraszthy, a Hungarian nobleman. The Count traveled throughout Europe to collect vine cuttings that became the origins of the Sonoma and Napa vineyards. In 1857, he founded the Buena Vista Winery, carving caves deep into the limestone hillside. These caves form the oldest winecellar in California. The ideal soil and weather conditions have enabled the region to produce world-class wines.

BUENA VISTA WINERY

Wine-making began in the Napa Valley in 1876 when Jacob Beringer founded his winery in St. Helena. It is the oldest continuously operating winery in the valley, remaining open through Prohibition by producing only "sacramental" wines. Beringer's home, a gothic Queen-Anne Victorian mansion (1883) features imported woodwork and stained glass windows made by San Francisco artisans in the 1880s.

Adjacent Greystone Cellars (1888) was at one time the largest winery in the world. It was built into the hillside to aid the winemaking process. Grapes were brought in on the third floor and crushed the juice drained to the second floor for fermenting, and then aged on the first. The winery, once belonging to Christian Brothers, has been purchased by the Culinary Institute for use as a cooking school. Another of the valley's first wineries is Inglenook Napa Valley in Rutherford. It was founded in 1879 by a Finnish sea captain, Gustav Niebaum. The chateau and wine cellars date from 1882. Near St. Helena, the **Silverado Museum** features original manuscripts, first editions and photographs by Robert Louis Stevenson.

COLONEL ALLENSWORTH S.H.P.

THE CENTRAL VALLEY

California's San Joaquin (*hwa-keen*) valley is over 300 miles long and 50 miles wide. Irrigated by the 440-mile California Aqueduct, it is the most productive agricultural region in the world, with more than a million acres of irrigated farmland. In Bakersfield, the **Kern County Museum** is nationally recognized for its outstanding preservation of historic buildings. Businesses, homes, and public buildings recreate life in Kern County between the 1860s and 1930s. **The California Living Museum** northeast of Bakersfield is a satellite natural history museum.

In Fresno, the largest city in San Joaquin Valley, two historic homes have been restored and operate as museums. The **Kearney Mansion Museum** (1901) contains its original furnishings and wall coverings imported from Europe. The **Meux Home Museum** (1888-89) is furnished with Victorian-era antiques.

The **Fort Miller Block House** in Fresno's Roeding Park presents exhibits of 19th-century frontier days.

Hanford was once home to one of the largest Chinese communities in California. An 1893 Taoist temple, which also served as a meeting hall and school, still stands in China Alley. **Courthouse Square**, in the heart of Hanford, has many original buildings.

In Modesto, the **McHenry Mansion and Museum** presents a number of dioramas from days past. Artifacts from local pioneers furnish a doctor's office, blacksmith shop, schoolroom, and general store, along with gold mining and fire fighting exhibits.

Many small towns such as Snelling have changed little in the last 100 years. Among its historic buildings are the original 1857 county courthouse. The town of Locke, built in 1915 by Chinese immigrants, retains its Old West appearance with buildings like the **Dai Loy Gambling House Museum** with original gaming tables.

The **Colonel Allensworth SHP** north of Bakersfield is the only California town established by African Americans. Col. Allensworth (1842-1914), a businessman and minister who fought in the Civil War, later became the highest ranking black officer of his time. He and Professor William Payne founded the town in 1908, thinking that a place free of discriminatory laws would promote "intellectual and industrial liberty" for black Americans. The park offers living history presentations.

The Deserts

Desolate and foreboding, California's deserts have attracted few settlers. In the 1880s, the discovery of gold and borax led to the establishment of mining towns, but most of these are now abandoned ghost towns. **Bodie SHP** is the best preserved ghost town in the desert. The lack of water (fewer than two inches of precipitation annually) and temperatures exceeding 115° in the summer down to freezing in the winter have proven an effective deterrent to civilization.

The Coachella Valley is one notable exception, owing to its protected location between the San Jacinto and San Bernardino Mountains, and the benefit of numerous natural springs. Over 350 days of sunshine a year have made Palm Springs, Cathedral City, Desert Hot Springs and Rancho Mirage popular destinations.

The **Indian Canyons**, the world's largest natural palm oases, are the ancestral home of the Agua Caliente band of Cahuilla Indians. Rock art, village sites and trails still exist on land owned by the Agua Calientes. The public Canyons house several endangered species of flora and fauna. When Ralph Belamy and Charlie Farrell opened The Racquet Club in 1936, Palm Springs became famous. **The Palm Springs Desert Museum**, opened in 1938 as a natural science museum, has since expanded its collections to include Native American (particularly Cahuilla Indian) artifacts and contemporary American and classic Western art.

The Living Desert wild animal park and botanical gardens, located on 1200 acres near Palm Desert, recreates eight of the world's unique desert environments. Bighorn sheep, zebras, gila monsters and other animals can he seen from nature trails. The best time to visit the desert is in early spring when the cacti bloom with an amazing array of colorful flowers.

Death Valley N.P.SCOTTY'S CASTLE

Scotty's Castle, located at the north end of Death Valley National Park, was constructed by local mining legend Walter Scott, a.k.a. "Death Valley Scotty", with funds from wealthy Chicago businessman, Albert Johnson, who planned the castle as a vacation retreat. Construction of the Mediterranean-styled hacienda was begun in 1922 at a cost of $2.4 million. Scotty, always the big talker, claimed the castle was his, and Johnson gamely went along with the story. When Johnson suffered financial ruin in the stock market crash of 1929, the project was abandoned. The castle remains unfinished, but it is beautifully decorated with fine furnishings and artwork. The elevations in Death Valley range from 282 feet below sea level to 11,049 feet above. Monitor the Park's weather reports closely.

The Mother Lode

Probably the most significant event in the development of California was the Gold Rush of 1849. The discovery of gold at Sutter's Mill lured thousands of prospectors from around the world. By 1900, more than 125 million ounces of gold had been mined from the Mother Lode, worth multi-billions in today's currency.

The Golden Chain Highway (Hwy. 49) follows the trail of the Forty-niners, connecting the mining towns along the foothills of the Sierra Nevada. From Oakdale to Portola, each town tells a part of gold rush history.

It was at Coloma on January 24, 1848, that James Marshall, a foreman for Capt. John Sutter, discovered gold while building a millrace on the American River. Although he and Sutter tried to keep the discovery a secret, word soon got out and the rush was on. By the summer of 1849, thousands of prospectors were scouring the foothills of the Sierra Nevada searching for gold. Sutter tried to evict the trespassers, and even took his case to Washington D.C., but his efforts were in vain. While an estimated $50 million was mined off his land, Sutter died years later a poor man.

MARSHALL GOLD DISCOVERY S.H.P.

The **Marshall Gold Discovery SHP** offers a reconstruction of Sutter's Mill and a statue of Marshall. The park encompasses the entire town of Coloma, preserved as it was during the mining days. The **Gold Discovery Museum** recounts the stories of Marshall and Sutter and presents an historical account of the gold rush, mining methods, and assaying equipment.

Columbia SHP is the largest fully operating gold rush town that has been preserved. After the fire of 1857, the town was rebuilt with brick and iron. Museums and displays such as the blacksmith shop inform visitors about frontier life in the 1860s. Local businesses like the Columbia Candy Kitchen preserve the Old West atmosphere. Activities include stagecoach rides and panning for gold.

COLUMBIA S.H.P.

Mariposa was one of the richest towns in the region, mining millions of dollars of gems and minerals from the surrounding hills. The **Mariposa Museum and History Center**, one of the best small museums in the country, provides an outstanding view of frontier life in a late 19th century mining town. An historic 1863 home and the old Mariposa *Gazette* building have been moved to the grounds. Displays depicting the sheriff's office, a millinery, pharmacy, miner's cabin, and lady's parlor are enhanced by diary entries, letters, price lists (e.g. Eggs, $3/each), and documents. Many items were donated by descendants of early Mariposa residents. An Indian village, carriage house, and mining equipment are also located on the grounds.

The **Mariposa County Courthouse**, built in 1854, is the state's oldest operating government building. The clock tower, added in 1866, was brought to California by sailing ship around Cape Horn.

Other sites in town include **St. Joseph's Catholic Church**, in continuous operation since 1863, and the **California State Mining and Mineral Museum**, the leading museum of its kind in the state. Specimens of historic interest are on display, such as the world's largest natural gold specimen, the 201.4 troy ounce Fricot Nugget. Jules Fricot purchased the nugget in 1878 for a mere $3,500.

The North Coast

The north coast of California is a truly spectacular sight. Hwy. 1 winds along rocky seaside cliffs, over coastal mountains, and through deep stands of 250-foot-tall redwoods. The first Europeans were English and Russian trappers who hunted sea otters, deer, elk, and bear. The discovery of gold in the 1850s brought miners to the Eureka, Crescent City and

EUREKA VICTORIAN

Shasta areas. When the mines were depleted, the settlers turned to logging and fishing, the North Coast's primary industries today.

Russia's southernmost outpost in the continental United States was **Fort Ross**, north of Jenner. The fortress was built in 1812 by hunters to support the sea otter trade. The state historic park contains a restored Russian Orthodox chapel, commandant's house, and museum which exhibits tools, firearms, and historic artifacts.

The Point Arena Lighthouse (1870) stands 115-feet above sea level and offers unsurpassed vistas. Tours are available. Inland from Point Arena on Highway 101 is the town of Ukiah, meaning "deep valley." **The Grace Hudson Museum** (1986) and **Sun House** (1911) is devoted to local art, history, and anthropology of the area and its Pomo Indians. Doctor Hudson devoted his life to collecting and studying North Coast Indian artworks and artifacts, and the museum possesses an outstanding collection of Indian basketry. Grace Hudson is renowned for her paintings of Pomo Indians. The Sun House is a Craftsman-style redwood bungalow which incorporates North Coast Indian elements. It has been named a California Historic Landmark.

Fort Bragg's **Guest House Museum** (1892) presents local history and a model of the old fort.

Mendocino, called the New England of the West Coast because of its Cape Cod-style architecture, is a popular

RUSSIAN ORTHODOX CHAPEL FORT ROSS S.H.P.

artists' colony. **The Kelley House Museum** is housed in a restored 1861 residence, surrounded by a lovely garden. Its library is rich in archives of local history.

The largest city on the North Coast is Eureka, meaning "I found it!" More than 100 restored Victorian homes include the extraordinary **Carson Mansion** (1885). In Old Town, the **Clarke Historical Museum** has a fine collection of Indian Basketry, ceremonial clothing and artifacts. Changing exhibits include Victorian and Humboldt County pioneer artifacts. The museum is in the former bank of Eureka, a historical building of marble and granite built in 1912 Italian-Renaissance style. **Fort Humboldt** (1853), once headquarters for General Ulysses S. Grant, is now a state park featuring historical exhibits on the logging industry.

To the north, in Crescent City, is **Battery Point Lighthouse**, one of the oldest on the Pacific coast. No longer run by the U.S. Coast Guard, it operates as a private aid to navigation. There is a museum and guided tours are offered in the summer.

YOSEMITE

Yosemite National Park became the first wilderness area set aside by any government when President Lincoln signed legislation in 1864 protecting the area. Its grandeur inspired preservationist John Muir to start the conservation movement and prompted Theodore Roosevelt to declare it "the most beautiful place on earth."

HALF DOME AND COOK'S MEADOW

In Yosemite Valley, the **Ahwahnee Hotel** (1927) has been designated a National Historic Landmark. Massive stone fireplaces, hardwood floors, cathedral ceilings, elegant furnishings and artworks are part of the luxury accommodations. Floor to ceiling windows frame views of the valley's most spectacular sites: Half Dome, Glacier Point and Yosemite Falls. Each year since its opening, the Ahwahnee has presented The Bracebridge Dinner, a Christmas pageant adapted from Washington Irving's "Sketch Book" of a Christmas Day in 1718 at Squire Bracebridge's Old English Manor. Traditional English carols, costumes, customs, a banquet, and entertainment by the Lord of Misrule, the Squire, and the Eugene Fulton Chorale relive eighteenth century Yuletide festivities.

At the south end of the park, **The Mariposa Grove Museum** presents exhibits on Giant sequoias, among the oldest and largest living things on earth. The **Pioneer Yosemite History Center** is staffed by costumed interpreters. Tourists first came to Yosemite in 1835 when a hotel was established at Wawona. Rebuilt, the **Wawona Hotel** is a National Historic Landmark, acclaimed for its beautifully restored Victorian interior.

National Historic Sites, Monuments and Parks

Alcatraz Island	San Francisco
Channel Islands National Park	Ventura
Death Valley National Park	Death Valley
Devils Postpile National Monument	near Mammoth Lakes
Eugene O'Neill National Historic Site	Danville
Fort Point National Historic Site	Presidio of San Francisco
John Muir National Historic Site	Martinez
Joshua Tree National Park	Twentynine Palms

LAKE ALMANOR, LASSEN VOLCANIC NATIONAL PARK

Lassen Volcanic National Park	Mineral
Lava Beds National Monument	Tulelake
Manzanar National Historic Site	Independence
Muir Woods National Monument	Mill Valley
Rosie the Riveter WWII Home Front NHP	Richmond
San Francisco Maritime NHP	San Francisco
Sequoia & Kings Canyon National Parks	Tulare and Fresno counties
Yosemite National Park	the Sierra Nevada

State Historic Monuments, Parks and Museums

Anderson Marsh SHP	Lake County
Antelope Valley Indian Museum	Los Angeles
Bale Grist Mill SHP	Napa
Benicia Capitol SHP	Solano
Bidwell Mansion SHP	Butte

BODE SHP

Bode SHP	Mono
California Citrus SHP	Riverside
California Mining & Mineral Museum	Mariposa
California State Railroad Museum	Sacramento
California State Capital Museum	Sacramento
Chumash Painted Cave SHP	Santa Barbara
Colonel Allensworth SHP	Tulare
Columbia SHP	Tuolumne
El Presidio de Santa Barbara SHP	Santa Barbara
Empire Mine SHP	Nevada

Folsom Powerhouse SHP	Sacramento
Fort Humboldt SHP	Humboldt
Fort Ross SHP	Sonoma
Fort Tejon SHP	Kern
Governor's Mansion SHP	Sacramento
Hearst San Simeon SHM	San Luis
Indian Grinding Rock SHP	Amador
Jack London SHP	Sonoma
La Purisima Mission SHP	Santa Barbara
Leland Stanford Mansion SHP	Sacramento
Los Encinos SHP	Los Angeles
Malakoff Diggins SHP	Nevada
Marconi Conference Center SHP	Marin
Marshall Gold Discovery SHP	El Dorado
Monterey SHP	Monterey
Old Sacramento SHP	Sacramento
Old Town San Diego SHP	San Diego
Olompali SHP	Marin
Petaluma Adobe SHP	Sonoma
Pigeon Point Light Station SHP	San Mateo
Pio Pico SHP	Los Angeles

POINT SUR SHP

Point Sur SHP	Monterey
Railtown 1897 SHP	Tuolumne
San Juan Bautista SHP	San Benito
San Pasqual Battlefield SHP	San Diego
Santa Cruz Mission SHP	Santa Cruz
Santa Susana Pass SHP	Los Angeles
Shasta SHP	Shasta
Sonoma SHP	Sonoma
State Indian Museum	Sacramento
Sutter's Fort SHP	Sacramento
Tomo-Kahni SHP	Kern
Wassama Round House SHP	Madera
Watts Towers of Simon Rodia SHP	Los Angeles
Weaverville Joss House SHP	Trinity
Will Rogers SHP	Los Angeles
William B. Ide Adobe SHP	Tehama
Woodland Opera House SHP	Yolo